BACKYARD WILDLIFE
Prairie Dogs

by Kristin Schuetz

BELLWETHER MEDIA · MINNEAPOLIS, MN

Note to Librarians, Teachers, and Parents:

Blastoff! Readers are carefully developed by literacy experts and combine standards-based content with developmentally appropriate text.

Level 1 provides the most support through repetition of high-frequency words, light text, predictable sentence patterns, and strong visual support.

Level 2 offers early readers a bit more challenge through varied simple sentences, increased text load, and less repetition of high-frequency words.

Level 3 advances early-fluent readers toward fluency through increased text and concept load, less reliance on visuals, longer sentences, and more literary language.

Level 4 builds reading stamina by providing more text per page, increased use of punctuation, greater variation in sentence patterns, and increasingly challenging vocabulary.

Level 5 encourages children to move from "learning to read" to "reading to learn" by providing even more text, varied writing styles, and less familiar topics.

Whichever book is right for your reader, Blastoff! Readers are the perfect books to build confidence and encourage a love of reading that will last a lifetime!

This edition first published in 2014 by Bellwether Media, Inc.

No part of this publication may be reproduced in whole or in part without written permission of the publisher. For information regarding permission, write to Bellwether Media, Inc., Attention: Permissions Department, 5357 Penn Avenue South, Minneapolis, MN 55419.

Library of Congress Cataloging-in-Publication Data

Schuetz, Kristin, author.
  Prairie Dogs / by Kristin Schuetz.
      pages cm. – (Blastoff! Readers. Backyard Wildlife)
  Summary: "Developed by literacy experts for students in kindergarten through grade three, this book introduces prairie dogs to young readers through leveled text and related photos"– Provided by publisher.
  Audience: Age 5-8.
  Audience: Grades K to 3.
  Includes bibliographical references and index.
  ISBN 978-1-60014-971-9 (hardcover : alk. paper)
  1. Prairie dogs–Juvenile literature. I. Title. II. Series: Blastoff! readers. 1, Backyard wildlife.
  QL737.R68S348 2014
  599.36'7–dc23

                                                                    2014000808

Contents

Prairie dogs are large **rodents**. They like to stand on their back feet.

Prairie dogs **scurry** around grasslands. Mounds of dirt mark their homes.

They dig **burrows** underground. These have bedrooms and bathrooms.

Burrows are often close together. These towns can stretch for miles.

Prairie dogs live
in family groups.
They **groom**
one another and
share meals.

Families **forage** for food above the ground. They **gnaw** on grasses, roots, and seeds.

Prairie dogs greet family members with a kiss. They chase away **outsiders**.

Prairie dogs watch out for **predators**. Hawks, coyotes, and snakes hunt them.

A **lookout** barks to warn others of danger. Into the burrows, prairie dogs!

Glossary

burrows—holes in the ground that some animals dig

forage—to search for food

gnaw—to bite or nibble on something for a long time

groom—to clean

lookout—an animal that watches for danger

outsiders—animals that do not belong to a certain group

predators—animals that hunt other animals for food

rodents—small animals with long front teeth that grow throughout life

scurry—to run around in a hurry

To Learn More

AT THE LIBRARY
Grucella, A.J. *Prairie Dogs in Danger*. New York, N.Y.: Gareth Stevens Publishing, 2014.

Magby, Meryl. *Prairie Dogs*. New York, N.Y.: PowerKids Press, 2012.

Phillips, Dee. *Prairie Dog's Hideaway*. New York, N.Y.: Bearport Pub., 2012.

ON THE WEB
Learning more about prairie dogs is as easy as 1, 2, 3.

1. Go to www.factsurfer.com.

2. Enter "prairie dogs" into the search box.

3. Click the "Surf" button and you will see a list of related web sites.

With factsurfer.com, finding more information is just a click away.

Index